The Fundamental Concepts of Object-Oriented Programming

Author: Dimitrios Kalemis

Copyright 2013

(This page is intentionally left blank)

Table of contents

Motivation

Unless someone spells out for you the fundamentals concepts of Object-Oriented Programming (OOP), you may have a difficult time grasping them. You need to know not only what those concepts are, but also what it is that makes them fundamental. You need to know the defining line between OOP and non-OOP. For example, where does structured programming ends and OOP begins? What is the defining line? When do we cross it? What makes OOP what it is? What do we gain when we do OOP? Is OOP really necessary? Are there any alternatives?

By the end of this book you will have a crystal clear view of the concepts behind OOP and will be able to understand where it fits in relation to other types of programming. You will be able to pinpoint the subtle defining lines that separate OOP from other types of programming and understand its usefulness and shortcomings.

This book is unique because it will give you an insightful perspective into OOP, based on the most fundamental concepts that led to its formation. The book's approach to OOP will be conceptual and historical at the same time, something that will give you great insight. It is likely that you will have many "a-ha moments" reading this book and, at the end, you may even reach a feeling of "enlightenment".

In the beginning

In the beginning, people used machine code. Then they replaced machine code with the assembly language. It was a big step forward. After that, another, greater step was the implementation of high-level instructions.

Instructions were assignments and formulas, logic statements (if-then-else), for loops, while loops, etc. But one of the instructions was found to be problematic. This was the goto statement. The ability to jump to whatever part of the program was found to produce complex, convoluted, "spaghetti" code. Thus, care was exercised so as to avoid and even eliminate the use of this instruction. All other instructions could be used and make up for the loss of goto. Goto is not needed to write programs and its use can lead to badly written software.

So, after that, people were happy that they had high-level instructions and not assembly language ones. They could program complex logic with few instructions, without caring much about the underlying machine implementation.

Programmers also though that they could put frequently used code in procedures and functions and call them whenever they were needed, instead of copying and pasting code around. This way, if the procedure or the function needed correction, it would be done in one place only (in the definition of the procedure or function). Also, the procedures and functions could be made to accept parameters and, thus, be called parametrically.

All those concepts predated the object-oriented programming paradigm. Up to this point I described how people programmed without knowing or using any of the concepts of OOP.

You can see that people had a lot of power in their hands with respect to ease and ability to create programs. They had high-level instructions and they could also combine them into reusable procedures and functions. This paradigm came to be known as structured programming. People that followed structured programming techniques avoided goto instructions. Instead they used the other available instructions to create procedures and functions. They then used these procedures and functions in order to create software code of a larger base (amount). This way they could tackle major software projects that involved the effort of many programmers.

A great language for un-structured programming was BASIC, at least its early versions. In early versions of BASIC, goto instructions were used for control flow, which led to "spaghetti" code. Great languages for structured programming were PASCAL and C. Later on, newer versions of BASIC obtained many of the traits of structured programming.

Up until now, no OOP programming concepts have been introduced in our discussion. So, if someone tells you that the concepts discussed here thus far are part of OOP, she may be incorrect. Although OOP produces nice "structured" programs, all concepts introduced here pertain to structured programming, not OOP. The use of procedures in order to reuse and maintain code is definitely a structured programming concept, not an OOP one.

Enter OOP

Ok, we saw that with structured programming, people had great power and ease. Their methodology for creating programs was sufficiently sound. And this methodology, this paradigm, still is great, even in our days. You can go a long way with structured programming.

But people discovered concepts and techniques that could further expand their ability to write good, clean, maintainable programs. Some of those concepts pertain to a programming philosophy, a programming paradigm that came to be known as object-oriented programming. The purpose of this book is to reveal the concepts behind this paradigm. And the first thing that has to be done is to clarify that OOP came after structured programming and introduced new concepts.

Again, you may see structured programming concepts like the use of procedures and functions being tossed around as OOP concepts. They are not. They are structured programming concepts. OOP has its own concepts and we are going to explore them. And we are also going to find and pinpoint the defining lines that separate structured programming from OOP.

So, let us begin.

Programming environment and data

I am going to use C++ for the examples and analysis in this book, since it can easily support from low-level to high-level programming and accommodate structured programming (C language style) as well as OOP (C++ language style).

I am going to present a few programs. Each program is in a file with the .cpp extension. I will show the source code from each .cpp file and after it, I will show the output we get from running the corresponding program. You can find these programs online, in my blog, at http://dkalemis.wordpress.com. In my blog, I have a page (not a blog post, but a page linked along the top menu) called "My books". There, under the title of this book, you will find a link from which you can download the source code, the compiled program and its output for each of the programs.

You can compile each .cpp file yourself, using your favorite C++ language and programming environment. For example, if you use Visual Studio, you should put each .cpp file in its own folder and then, from Visual Studio, you should create a "project from existing code", defining the folder that you put the .cpp file and defining the actual .cpp file, as well. You will choose "Visual C++" as the programming language and you will choose to create a "console application project". Then you will build and run the project.

As you will see, at the beginning of each program, I use the following code

```
# include <iostream>
using namespace std;
```

Depending on your C++ language implementation, you might need to slightly change those lines. Some implementations, for example, would like you to write <iostream.h> instead of <iostream>.

You will also notice, that in the first two programs I use the instruction

```
cout.imbue(locale(""));
```

This is because, depending on the particular system, this instruction may help to give a nice format when displaying numbers. For example, an integer number such as 12345678 will be displayed as 12,345,678.

Because we will need an example and some data in our programs, I thought we could do a rudimentary study of New York's five boroughs.

From Wikipedia, we get the following information about the five boroughs of New York, in a nicely formatted table:

New York's five boroughs overview				
Jurisdiction		**Population**	**Land area**	
Borough	*County*	*1 July 2012 Estimates*	*square miles*	*square km*
Manhattan	New York	1,619,090	23	59
The Bronx	Bronx	1,408,473	42	109
Brooklyn	Kings	2,565,635	71	183
Queens	Queens	2,272,771	109	283
Staten Island	Richmond	470,728	58	151
City of New York		**8,336,697**	**303**	**786**
State of New York		19,570,261	47,214	122,284
Source: United States Census Bureau[1][2][3]				

To visualize where the five boroughs lie, Wikipedia provides us with the following map:

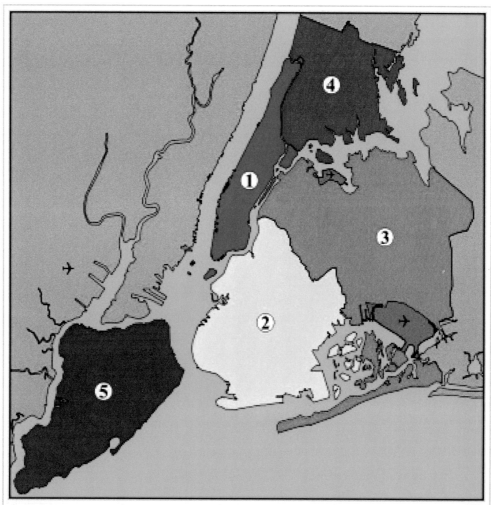

The Five Boroughs of New York City: **1: Manhattan,** 2: Brooklyn, 3: Queens, **4: The Bronx,** and **5: Staten Island** (airports are within Queens).

Parallel arrays

So, let us take the data from Wikipedia's table and see if we can use it in a program.

Program 1 – source code

```cpp
# include <iostream>
using namespace std;

void main(void)
{
    cout.imbue(locale(""));

    char * borough [5];
    char * county[5];
    int population[5];
    int landareasm[5];

    borough[0] = "Manhattan";
    county[0] = "New York";
    population[0] = 1619090;
    landareasm[0] = 23;

    borough[1] = "The Bronx";
    county[1] = "Bronx";
    population[1] = 1408473;
    landareasm[1] = 42;

    borough[2] = "Brooklyn";
    county[2] = "Kings";
    population[2] = 2565635;
    landareasm[2] = 71;

    borough[3] = "Queens";
    county[3] = "Queens";
    population[3] = 2272771;
```

```
landareasm[3] = 109;

borough[4] = "Staten Island";
county[4] = "Richmond";
population[4] = 470728;
landareasm[4] = 58;

int sumOfPopulation;
int sumOfLandAreaInSM;

sumOfPopulation = 0;
sumOfLandAreaInSM = 0;

for (int i = 0; i < 5; i++)
{
    cout << "The borough of "
         << borough[i]
         << " is in the county of "
         << county[i]
         << " and has a population of "
         << population[i]
         << " people"
         << " and a land area of "
         << landareasm[i]
         << " square miles."
         << endl;

    sumOfPopulation = sumOfPopulation +
                      population[i];
    sumOfLandAreaInSM = sumOfLandAreaInSM +
                        landareasm[i];
}

cout << endl;
cout << "The City of New York"
     << " consists of these five boroughs"
     << " and has a total population of "
     << sumOfPopulation
     << " people"
     << " and a total square area of "
     << sumOfLandAreaInSM
     << " square miles."
     << endl;
}
```

Program 1 – output

```
The borough of Manhattan is in the county of New
York and has a population of 1,619,090 people and
a land area of 23 square miles.
The borough of The Bronx is in the county of
Bronx and has a population of 1,408,473 people
and a land area of 42 square miles.
The borough of Brooklyn is in the county of Kings
and has a population of 2,565,635 people and a
land area of 71 square miles.
The borough of Queens is in the county of Queens
and has a population of 2,272,771 people and a
land area of 109 square miles.
The borough of Staten Island is in the county of
Richmond and has a population of 470,728 people
and a land area of 58 square miles.

The City of New York consists of these five
boroughs and has a total population of 8,336,697
people and a total square area of 303 square
miles.
```

What we did in Program 1, is that we created four "parallel" arrays (borough, county, population, landareasm).

```
char * borough [5];
char * county[5];
int population[5];
int landareasm[5];
```

The word "parallel" here has the meaning of "independent". Each array is independent from the other arrays, and we can understand its relationship to the other three arrays only in our brains. The compiler and programming language have no notion of the relationship of the four arrays.

So, here each array holds the corresponding data for all boroughs. For example, the array named "population" holds the population for each of the five boroughs.

To access the information for each borough, we use an index. We have arranged things neatly, so that the same index corresponds to the same borough. Index 0, for example, corresponds to the New York borough, in all four arrays.

That was the way people used to program in the beginning, before any concept of object-orientation existed.

Well, Program 1 is neat and nicely organized, but something bothered people. When you program this way, you have each borough's data scattered among the four arrays. Your information is arranged by attribute (county or population) rather by borough.

Of course, you have each borough symbolized by an index, here named i and going from 0 to 4. But people wanted each borough's data to be together. They wanted things arranged not by attribute but by object, the object here being each borough. People thought that programs would be better this way, in terms of ease of coding and ease of understanding the code.

Structures

So people invented the concept of structures. A structure is a user-defined type that has one or more of pieces of information bound together.

Let us see how Program 1 can be rewritten with the use of a structure.

Program 2 – source code

```
# include <iostream>
using namespace std;

void main(void)
{
    cout.imbue(locale(""));

    struct borough
    {
        char * name;
        char * county;
        int population;
        int landareasm;
    };

    struct borough boroughs[5];

    boroughs[0].name = "Manhattan";
    boroughs[0].county = "New York";
    boroughs[0].population = 1619090;
    boroughs[0].landareasm = 23;

    boroughs[1].name = "The Bronx";
```

```cpp
boroughs[1].county = "Bronx";
boroughs[1].population = 1408473;
boroughs[1].landareasm = 42;

boroughs[2].name = "Brooklyn";
boroughs[2].county = "Kings";
boroughs[2].population = 2565635;
boroughs[2].landareasm = 71;

boroughs[3].name = "Queens";
boroughs[3].county = "Queens";
boroughs[3].population = 2272771;
boroughs[3].landareasm = 109;

boroughs[4].name = "Staten Island";
boroughs[4].county = "Richmond";
boroughs[4].population = 470728;
boroughs[4].landareasm = 58;

int sumOfPopulation;
int sumOfLandAreaInSM;

sumOfPopulation = 0;
sumOfLandAreaInSM = 0;

for (int i = 0; i < 5; i++)
{
    cout << "The borough of "
         << boroughs[i].name
         << " is in the county of "
         << boroughs[i].county
         << " and has a population of "
         << boroughs[i].population
         << " people"
         << " and a land area of "
         << boroughs[i].landareasm
         << " square miles."
         << endl;

    sumOfPopulation = sumOfPopulation +
                    boroughs[i].population;
    sumOfLandAreaInSM = sumOfLandAreaInSM +
                    boroughs[i].landareasm;
}
```

```
    cout << endl;
    cout << "The City of New York"
        << " consists of these five boroughs"
        << " and has a total population of "
        << sumOfPopulation
        << " people"
        << " and a total square area of "
        << sumOfLandAreaInSM
        << " square miles."
        << endl;
}
```

Program 2 – output

The borough of Manhattan is in the county of New
York and has a population of 1,619,090 people and
a land area of 23 square miles.
The borough of The Bronx is in the county of
Bronx and has a population of 1,408,473 people
and a land area of 42 square miles.
The borough of Brooklyn is in the county of Kings
and has a population of 2,565,635 people and a
land area of 71 square miles.
The borough of Queens is in the county of Queens
and has a population of 2,272,771 people and a
land area of 109 square miles.
The borough of Staten Island is in the county of
Richmond and has a population of 470,728 people
and a land area of 58 square miles.

The City of New York consists of these five
boroughs and has a total population of 8,336,697
people and a total square area of 303 square
miles.

The output of Program 2 is exactly the
same as the output of Program 1. But
Program 2 has a fundamental

difference. In Program 2 we did away with the creation of "parallel" arrays. In Program 2 we have only one array, named "boroughs". This array contains structures. So we have an array of structures.

The structures are of type borough

```
struct borough
{
    char * name;
    char * county;
    int population;
    int landareasm;
};
```

Each borough structure has a pointer to a name, a pointer to a county, an integer population and an integer land area measured in square meters.

All data for each borough is contained in a borough structure. So it is not scattered in different arrays, as was the case in Program 1.

People really like having all data of a thing, an object, an entity together. It makes things easier to understand and handle.

Of course, the same amount of information that we had in Program 1, we also have in Program 2. For each borough we track its name, county, population and land area in square meters. Because we have 5 boroughs, we have 5 * 4 = 20 pieces of information. So we have 20 pieces of information in Program 1 and also in Program 2. But we organize this information in a different manner in Program 2. We hold all data of each borough together and we separate each borough from the other boroughs. We bring all boroughs together using an array, named "boroughs".

The concept of the structure is a very powerful one. It characterizes an object and holds together its data.

This was the first step towards object-oriented programming: the concept of the structure, the concept of holding all data of an object together.

So, is this the defining line because structured programming and object-oriented programming? Is creating structures for objects what enters us into the realm of OOP?

Well, although this is the first step into OOP, hardly anyone thinks structures and holding data together as the defining line between structured programming and OOP. Everyone considers the concept of a structure to be a concept of structured programming.

So, even though this was a first big step towards OOP, the fact that we have structures in our program does not yet enter us into the realm of OOP.

So, let us continue.

In Program 3, we calculate the land area in square kilometers from the land area in square miles.

Program 3 – source code

```
# include <cmath>
# include <iostream>
using namespace std;

struct borough
{
   char * name;
   char * county;
   int population;
   int landareasm;
};

int calculate_landareask (struct borough
aBorough)
{
   return int(floor(2.58998811 *
            aBorough.landareasm + 0.5));
}
```

```cpp
void main(void)
{
    cout.imbue(locale(""));

    struct borough boroughs[5];

    boroughs[0].name = "Manhattan";
    boroughs[0].county = "New York";
    boroughs[0].population = 1619090;
    boroughs[0].landareasm = 23;

    boroughs[1].name = "The Bronx";
    boroughs[1].county = "Bronx";
    boroughs[1].population = 1408473;
    boroughs[1].landareasm = 42;

    boroughs[2].name = "Brooklyn";
    boroughs[2].county = "Kings";
    boroughs[2].population = 2565635;
    boroughs[2].landareasm = 71;

    boroughs[3].name = "Queens";
    boroughs[3].county = "Queens";
    boroughs[3].population = 2272771;
    boroughs[3].landareasm = 109;

    boroughs[4].name = "Staten Island";
    boroughs[4].county = "Richmond";
    boroughs[4].population = 470728;
    boroughs[4].landareasm = 58;

    for (int i = 0; i < 5; i++)
    {
        cout << "The borough of "
             << boroughs[i].name
             << " has a land area of "
             << boroughs[i].landareasm
             << " square miles"
             << " which is equal to "
             << calculate_landareask(boroughs[i])
             << " square kilometers."
             << endl;
    }
}
```

Program 3 – output

```
The borough of Manhattan has a land area of 23
square miles which is equal to 60 square
kilometers.
The borough of The Bronx has a land area of 42
square miles which is equal to 109 square
kilometers.
The borough of Brooklyn has a land area of 71
square miles which is equal to 184 square
kilometers.
The borough of Queens has a land area of 109
square miles which is equal to 282square
kilometers.
The borough of Staten Island has a land area of
58 square miles which is equal to 150 square
kilometers.
```

In the first line of Program 3 I use the directive

```
# include <cmath>
```

because I will use cmath's function floor() in the calculations. Actually, it would have been straightforward to use the function round(), but some cmath implementations do not provide a round() function. Thus I use the expression

```
int(floor(something + 0.5))
```

where something is a real number, to make up for not being able to use the expression
`round(someting).`
Be warned that the way I use the floor() function here may provide the correct results, but it is not the correct way to derive the round() function, especially when negative numbers are involved (not the case here).

As we see in Program 3, we calculate the land area in square kilometers using the function
`int calculate_landareask (struct borough aBorough)`

We call the function, passing it the borough we want the function to operate on in each particular case:
`calculate_landareask(boroughs[i])`

We see that we get slightly different results than what the table from Wikipedia holds for the land areas in square kilometers. I attribute these discrepancies to the fact that both the values for the areas in miles and the areas in squares kilometers must have been calculated, then rounded and then added to the table. So, our calculations should be a little bit off, since we are using the table's rounded values of the land areas in square miles.

Program 3 is a program that adheres to the structured programming paradigm. It is as structured as they come. It uses the function calculate_landareask() to calculate the land area in square kilometers. The logic for this calculation exists neatly within this function.

Classes and objects

Whereas Program 3 is a perfect example of structured programming, people wanted more neatness. So they came up with a construct that they named "class". Program 4 is written using a class instead of structure. The class is named CBorough and provides the "blueprint" for each borough. From this class, we instantiate 5 objects, one for each borough. The output of program 4 is exactly the same as that of Program 3. But there is a big difference in Program 4, a big step towards OOP, waiting for us to spot it.

Program 4 – source code

```
# include <cmath>
# include <iostream>
using namespace std;

void main(void)
{
    cout.imbue(locale(""));
```

```cpp
class CBorough
{
public:
    char * name;
    char * county;
    int population;
    int landareasm;
    int calculate_landareask()
    {
        return int(floor(2.58998811 *
                   landareasm + 0.5));
    };
};

CBorough boroughs[5];

boroughs[0].name = "Manhattan";
boroughs[0].county = "New York";
boroughs[0].population = 1619090;
boroughs[0].landareasm = 23;

boroughs[1].name = "The Bronx";
boroughs[1].county = "Bronx";
boroughs[1].population = 1408473;
boroughs[1].landareasm = 42;

boroughs[2].name = "Brooklyn";
boroughs[2].county = "Kings";
boroughs[2].population = 2565635;
boroughs[2].landareasm = 71;

boroughs[3].name = "Queens";
boroughs[3].county = "Queens";
boroughs[3].population = 2272771;
boroughs[3].landareasm = 109;

boroughs[4].name = "Staten Island";
boroughs[4].county = "Richmond";
boroughs[4].population = 470728;
boroughs[4].landareasm = 58;

for (int i = 0; i < 5; i++)
{
```

```
        cout << "The borough of "
            << boroughs[i].name
            << " has a land area of "
            << boroughs[i].landareasm
            << " square miles"
            << " which is equal to "
            << boroughs[i].calculate_landareask()
            << " square kilometers."
            << endl;
    }
}
```

Program 4 – output

```
The borough of Manhattan has a land area of 23
square miles which is equal to 60 square
kilometers.
The borough of The Bronx has a land area of 42
square miles which is equal to 109 square
kilometers.
The borough of Brooklyn has a land area of 71
square miles which is equal to 184 square
kilometers.
The borough of Queens has a land area of 109
square miles which is equal to 282square
kilometers.
The borough of Staten Island has a land area of
58 square miles which is equal to 150 square
kilometers.
```

As I mentioned, the output of Program 4 is the same as that of Program 3. But the difference is that in Program 4 we use a class (named "CBorough") instead of a structure.

From the class CBorough we instantiate 5 objects and we keep them in the array "boroughs". This is done with the single statement:

```
CBorough boroughs[5];
```

The class contains the method (i.e. member function) calculate_landareask(). No longer is the calculate_landareask() globally visible. It is now accessible only through a borough object and it operates on the data of this object alone.

With structures, we had created a gathering of data. Now, with classes, we include in this gathering the very methods (member functions) that manipulate the data.

This is very powerful concept and a big step over Program 3. And the difference comes down to this: instead

of using Program 3's way of running
the calculation code:

```
calculate_landareask(boroughs[i])
```

we now use Program 4's way of
running the calculation code:

```
boroughs[i].calculate_landareask()
```

This is the big step forward that I wrote
that was waiting for us to spot it in the
program. This concept may amount to a
small change in notation, but is a great
step forward, indeed. To be able to
have classes that bring together data
and the code that manipulates them and
to be able to write **object.method**()
instead of **function(object)** to run the
code, is a major step towards the
essence and usefulness of OOP. (And
to be perfectly clear, method is the
function that is a member function, i.e.
it is declared inside the class).

Encapsulation and access specifiers

Indeed, the people that came up with the OOP concepts, wanted to achieve this exactly. They wanted to create objects, where each object would encompass all information about itself and all methods (algorithms) that are needed to get, set and manipulate this information.

Encapsulation is thought to be the encompassing of all data and methods inside an object. An object has attributes, i.e. data that define its state. These are the object's data members. Also, an object has methods that manipulate these data members, i.e. its state. These methods are the object's member functions.

Thus, an object's data is its state and implemented with data members and an object's methods are its behavior and implemented with member functions (methods).

There are two methods that are particularly helpful in many cases, the constructor and the destructor. In C++, the constructor is a method with the same name as the class and the destructor has the same name but preceded with a tilde (~). The constructor is called as soon as an object of the class is instantiated. In the constructor, the developer provides setup code for the object. The destructor is called as soon as the object is destroyed. In the destructor, the developer provides clean up code for the object. Not all classes need constructors or destructors, but many do.

As we saw, a class has data members and member functions. These can have different access specifiers. There are three access specifiers/keywords: private, protected and public.

 "Protected" will be discussed when we will talk about inheritance. "Private" are those data members and member functions that can only be accessed "inside the object" by the object's member functions. "Public are those data members and member functions that can be accessed by every other object, too.

According to the OO philosophy, all data members of an object should be private. Some of its member functions that are needed only by other member functions should be private as well. Lastly, the remaining member functions that should be called from other objects should be public.

An example of the definition of an object follows:

```
// Class declaration

Class CMyClass
{
:private
    // The state,
    // i.e data,
    // i.e. data members
    int dataMember1;
    double dataMember2;

    // Private behavior,
    // i.e private member functions
    // i.e. private methods
    char * memberFunctionX(…);
    int memberFunctionY(…);

:public
    // Public behavior,
    // i.e. public methods
    void memberFunction1(…);
    int memberFunction2(…);
};

// Class definition

    // Here we define the code
    // for the member functions
    …

// Object instantiation
```

```
// Here we create an object
//of class CMyClass

CMyClass myObject;
```

For an object to be instantiated, a class has to be declared and defined first. Then, we can instantiate as many objects of this class as we want. The class is the "blueprint". The objects that we instantiate from the class will essentially do the work of running their code.

In the example above, myObject has state that is private (dataMember1, dataMember2) and behavior that is public (memberFunction1, memberFunction2). The public member functions in their code can access the private data members and the private member functions (memberFunctionX, memberFunctionY) in order to do their work of providing the behavior of the object and to manage its state.

All other objects and all other code, in general, can only call the public methods (memberFunction1, memberFunction2) as follows:

Some code somewhere outside the class:

```
myObject.memberFunction1(…);
int i;
i = myObject.memberFunction2(…);
```

The people that came up with OOP imagined that a class will be the blueprint that will be used when the programmer instantiates one or more objects of this class. When we declare an integer

```
int myInt;
```

myInt takes everything from the int specification. The same happens when we instantiate an object of a class

```
CMyClass myObject;
```

myObject takes everything from the CMyClass specification: all data members and all member functions, with the access specifiers that CMyClass defines.

Thus, a class can also be thought of as a user-defined data type. Of course, a structure can also be thought as a user-defined data type. But a class is so much more powerful, since it encapsulates all data and methods of an entity.

Message passing

The people that came up with OOP also imagined method calling as message passing. This means that information and control passes from object to object when the code runs. But the code exists in the methods of objects. So, while an object1's method1 is running, this method might have a statement like object5.method21(…). In effect, the object5's method21 is called, with the necessary parameters. Since the call originates from object1's method1, OOP conceptually treats this as if object1 passes a message to object5, the message being the name of object5's method and the necessary parameters. Again, the message is passed from object1 to object5 and the message is only the name of object5's method and the corresponding parameters. The code for method21 is tucked inside object5.

Now, when object5's method21 runs, this method may call object3's method7 like so: object3.method7(…). This time it is object5 that passes a message to object3. The message is just the name of the method to be called with the necessary parameters: "method7(…)".

Of course, object1, object5 and object3 need not belong to the same class.

So, conceptually, OOP is about message passing between objects. This is why Program 4 is a big step towards OOP.

Although scholars would certainly disagree, I would dare to draw the line here and say that this point is the dividing line between structured programming and OOP. I would argue that the essence of OOP is a) the ability to hold together in a class both data and the corresponding code and b) the ability to write **object.method**() instead of **function(object).** Even though the algorithm in the method and the function are essentially the same, the small difference in notation constitutes a paradigm shift, that from structured programming to OOP.

In the preceding paragraph, I wrote that scholars would disagree and, indeed, scholars set the bar, the defining line between structured programming and OOP, higher, so to speak. They want to achieve much more from the OOP concept. Specifically, they want to be able to have inheritance. But not just inheritance; they want to have inheritance that also respects the

Liskov substitution principle. So, I am going to explain the concept of inheritance and the concept of the Liskov substitution principle. After I do this, you will know all the fundamental concepts of OOP and you will also know where scholars set the defining line between structured programming and OOP.

Inheritance

Earlier on we saw how a class provides the mold, the blueprint of how objects from this class should be created (instantiated). Sometimes, we may already have a class, say Class1 and we may also need a class, say Class2 that has everything Class1 has and even more. Thus, if Class1 has 5 data members and 10 methods, we would like Class2 to have all these data members and methods and also some new ones. We can easily create Class2 by copying all data members and methods from Class1 and then add the new data members and methods. But this would result in duplicated code, the duplicated code being all the data members and methods from Class1.

Instead, we can use inheritance. That is, we can create a Class2 that inherits from Class1. When we say that a class inherits from another, we mean that it inherits everything; all data members and methods. So, we need to specify the class (known as base or parent) from which the new class (known as derived or child) inherits, and we also need to specify the new data members and methods of the derived class. So, we are spared from having to duplicate everything from the base class.

Of course, entire class hierarchies can be made this way. From a base class, one or more classes can be derived. From each of these classes, zero or more classes can be derived and so on. The following image shows a very simple hierarchy. A base class called CBase is the parent. CBase has two children: the classes CDerived1 and

CDerived2. CDerived1 inherits from CBase and the same also holds true for CDerived2.

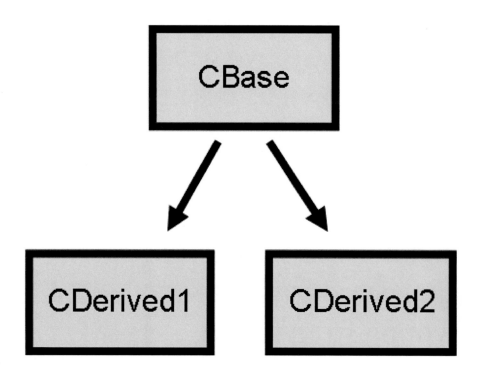

There is also the concept of multiple inheritance. According to this concept, a class may inherit from more than one base class, thus, a class may have more than one parents. This concept though is not considered fundamental, and scholars do not list it as mandatory in order to consider a language as OO. Instead, scholars find that multiple inheritance may sometimes lead to programs that are difficult to understand, so one should be cautious when using multiple inheritance. C++ supports multiple inheritance. We will not be talking much about multiple inheritance below, since it is not a fundamental or mandatory concept of OOP.

Remember when we talked about access specifiers (private, protected and public)? I did not explain what "protected" stands for, because it has to do with inheritance. Now I can explain it. If ClassX inherits from ClassA, then ClassX cannot access the private members of ClassA, but it can access the protected and public members of ClassA. The outside world cannot access the private and protected members of ClassA. Thus, protected are those members that are intended to be accessed from derived classes.

Program 5 implements the hierarchy that is depicted in the previous picture. We create (instantiate) one object of the base class CBase, called baseThing. We also create one object of the derived class CDerived1, called derived1Thing. And we also create one object of the derived class CDerived2, called derived2Thing.

Program 5 – source code

```
# include <iostream>
using namespace std;

void main(void)
{
   class CBase
   {
   public:
      void speak(void)
      {
         cout << "This is a Base object."
               << endl;
      };
```

```cpp
};

class CDerived1 : public CBase
{
public:
    void speak(void)
    {
        cout << "This is a Derived1 object."
            << endl;
    };
};

class CDerived2 : public CBase
{
public:
    void speak(void)
    {
        cout << "This is a Derived2 object."
            << endl;
    };
};

CBase baseThing;
CDerived1 derived1Thing;
CDerived2 derived2Thing;

cout << "Objects will now be accessed"
    << " directly."
    << endl;
baseThing.speak();
derived1Thing.speak();
derived2Thing.speak();

cout << "Objects will now be accessed"
    << " by a base pointer."
    << endl;
CBase * myBasePointer;
myBasePointer = &baseThing;
myBasePointer->speak();
myBasePointer = &derived1Thing;
myBasePointer->speak();
myBasePointer = &derived2Thing;
myBasePointer->speak();
}
```

Program 5 – output

```
Objects will now be accessed directly.
This is a Base object.
This is a Derived1 object.
This is a Derived2 object.
Objects will now be accessed by a base pointer.
This is a Base object.
This is a Base object.
This is a Base object.
```

As we see from the output of Program 5, when we access the derived objects directly, they behave as they should, that is, their methods are called. This means that the concept of hierarchy is implemented in this case. But when we access the derived objects via a pointer of the base class, they do not behave correctly. Instead, the base class method is called in each one. In other words, the last two lines in the output should have been:

```
This is a Derived1 object.
This is a Derived2 object.
```

This means that although the concept hierarchy works here, the Liskov substitution principle is not respected.

The Liskov substitution principle

The Liskov substitution principle states that we should be able to access a derived object via a pointer to its base class and the object should be able to function correctly.

I will explain this a little bit more: we can access an object and its methods using a pointer that has the type of the object's class. The object will behave correctly, calling its methods.

```
CDerived1 myDerived1Object;
CDerived1 * pD;
pD = &myDerived1Object
pD -> speak();
```

The last statement will call the derived method. Indeed, this is what we want to happen.

But what will it happen when we have the following code:

```
CDerived1 myDerived1Object;
CBase * pB;
pB = &myDerived1Object
pB -> speak();
```

The last statement should call the derived method. At least that is what the Liskov substitution principle demands. But as we saw, instead of the derived class method, the base class method is called instead.

So, Program 5 provides an example where the OO principle of hierarchy works, but the more advanced Liskov substitution principle does not.

Program 6 follows, in which both hierarchy and the Liskov substitution principle are respected, thus we reach our goal: to arrive at the defining line of OOP. Program 6 is a true OO program, a program that adheres to all fundamental OO principles.

Program 6 – source code

```cpp
# include <iostream>
using namespace std;

void main(void)
{
    class CBase
    {
    public:
        virtual void speak(void)
        {
            cout << "This is a Base object."
                << endl;
        };
    };

    class CDerived1 : public CBase
    {
    public:
        void speak(void)
        {
            cout << "This is a Derived1 object."
                << endl;
        };
    };

    class CDerived2 : public CBase
    {
    public:
        void speak(void)
        {
            cout << "This is a Derived2 object."
                << endl;
        };
    };

    CBase baseThing;
```

```
    CDerived1 derived1Thing;
    CDerived2 derived2Thing;

    cout << "Objects will now be accessed"
         << " directly."
         << endl;
    baseThing.speak();
    derived1Thing.speak();
    derived2Thing.speak();

    cout << "Objects will now be accessed"
         << " by a base pointer."
         << endl;
    CBase * myBasePointer;
    myBasePointer = &baseThing;
    myBasePointer->speak();
    myBasePointer = &derived1Thing;
    myBasePointer->speak();
    myBasePointer = &derived2Thing;
    myBasePointer->speak();
}
```

Program 6 – output

```
Objects will now be accessed directly.
This is a Base object.
This is a Derived1 object.
This is a Derived2 object.
Objects will now be accessed by a base pointer.
This is a Base object.
This is a Derived1 object.
This is a Derived2 object.
```

Program 6 is exactly like Program 5, except from the fact that Program 6 has one more word, the word "virtual" in the beginning of the declaration of the method speak() in the base class.

This makes all the difference. By adding the "virtual" specifier in front of the methods that we want to override (redefine) in derived classes, we make the program adhere not only to inheritance, but also to the Liskov substitution principle.

Ok, certainly scholars are right demanding that OO implementations include inheritance. After all, inheritance is all about the DRY (Don't Repeat Yourself) principle. By inheriting code, you avoid copying it and you have only one place where this code is defined. But what is this obsession that scholars have about the Liskov substitution principle? Why scholars are so obsessed with it and why do they demand that every OO implementation respects it? Why is the

Liskov substitution principle important?

Well, once you have understood the importance of the Liskov substitution principle, you will have achieved enlightenment, as far as OOP is concerned. So, let me explain the importance of this principle.

The importance of the Liskov substitution principle

Many times in programming we come at a situation where we have multiple objects and we want to be able to iterate over them and perform operations to each one. And usually these objects are instantiated from classes that belong to same hierarchy.

Let us take, for example, the hierarchy depicted in the last image. There might be a situation where we have a number of objects, some instantiated from CBase, some from CDerived1 and some from CDerived2. But we want to treat all of them irrespectively.

Such a situation is depicted in Program 7.

Program 7 – source code

```
# include <iostream>
using namespace std;

void main(void)
{
    class CBase
    {
    public:
        virtual void speak(void)
        {
            cout << "This is a Base object."
                << endl;
        };
    };

    class CDerived1 : public CBase
    {
    public:
        void speak(void)
        {
            cout << "This is a Derived1 object."
                << endl;
        };
    };

    class CDerived2 : public CBase
    {
    public:
        void speak(void)
        {
            cout << "This is a Derived2 object."
                << endl;
        };
    };

    CBase * myBasePointers[100];

    for (int i = 0; i< 100; i++)
    {
        if (i%3 == 0)
        {
            myBasePointers[i] = new CBase();
```

```
        }

        if (i%3 == 1)
        {
            myBasePointers[i] = new CDerived1();
        }

        if (i%3 == 2)
        {
            myBasePointers[i] = new CDerived2();
        }
    }

    for (int i = 0; i< 100; i++)
    {
        myBasePointers[i]->speak();
    }

    for (int i = 0; i< 100; i++)
    {
        delete myBasePointers[i];
    }
}
```

Program 7 – output

```
This is a Base object.
This is a Derived1 object.
This is a Derived2 object.
This is a Base object.
This is a Derived1 object.
This is a Derived2 object.
This is a Base object.
This is a Derived1 object.
This is a Derived2 object.
This is a Base object.
This is a Derived1 object.
This is a Derived2 object.
This is a Base object.
This is a Derived1 object.
This is a Derived2 object.
This is a Base object.
This is a Derived1 object.
This is a Derived2 object.
```

```
This is a Base object.
This is a Derived1 object.
This is a Derived2 object.
This is a Base object.
This is a Derived1 object.
This is a Derived2 object.
This is a Base object.
This is a Derived1 object.
This is a Derived2 object.
This is a Base object.
This is a Derived1 object.
This is a Derived2 object.
This is a Base object.
This is a Derived1 object.
This is a Derived2 object.
This is a Base object.
This is a Derived1 object.
This is a Derived2 object.
This is a Base object.
This is a Derived1 object.
This is a Derived2 object.
This is a Base object.
This is a Derived1 object.
This is a Derived2 object.
This is a Base object.
This is a Derived1 object.
This is a Derived2 object.
This is a Base object.
This is a Derived1 object.
This is a Derived2 object.
This is a Base object.
This is a Derived1 object.
This is a Derived2 object.
This is a Base object.
This is a Derived1 object.
This is a Derived2 object.
This is a Base object.
This is a Derived1 object.
This is a Derived2 object.
This is a Base object.
This is a Derived1 object.
```

```
This is a Derived2 object.
This is a Base object.
This is a Derived1 object.
This is a Derived2 object.
This is a Base object.
This is a Derived1 object.
This is a Derived2 object.
This is a Base object.
This is a Derived1 object.
This is a Derived2 object.
This is a Base object.
This is a Derived1 object.
This is a Derived2 object.
This is a Base object.
This is a Derived1 object.
This is a Derived2 object.
This is a Base object.
This is a Derived1 object.
This is a Derived2 object.
This is a Base object.
This is a Derived1 object.
This is a Derived2 object.
This is a Base object.
This is a Derived1 object.
This is a Derived2 object.
This is a Base object.
This is a Derived1 object.
This is a Derived2 object.
This is a Base object.
This is a Derived1 object.
This is a Derived2 object.
This is a Base object.
This is a Derived1 object.
This is a Derived2 object.
This is a Base object.
```

In Program 7, we create 100 objects. Some of them are CBase objects, some of them are CDerived1 objects and some of them are CDerived2 objects. Although we create them in a particular way (one CBase object, then one CDerived1 object, then one CDerived2 object, then one CBase object and so on), the program does not know before hand what kind of object in the hierarchy it will get. The objects are created dynamically. Although we can track them in our mind, the array we use and the base pointer we use to iterate over the array have no notion of the exact class that the each object is instantiated from.

All the program has to do is access all these objects that belong to the same hierarchy by using a pointer to iterate over all of them. The pointer should be of the same type as the base class. But then, how the pointer would know if it accesses an object from the base class or an object further down the hierarchy? The answer is that the pointer does not know, nor should it know. The pointer blindly references an object and it is up to the object to respect its functionality and act as it is supposed to act.

And each object is supposed to run its own method, when this method is called. Even if an object is referenced by a base class pointer, the object should call its derived method, if such method exists, instead of calling the base class method. We saw the correct behavior when we added the "virtual" keyword specifier in Program 6. The same holds true for Program 7. Because we added the virtual keyword in Program 7 as well, the objects behave correctly. That means that even though they are accessed via a base class pointer, their correct method is called.

We can examine that this is so by observing the output of Program 7.

Such situations come up in many programs. Many times we have objects that are not all of the same class but that belong to the same hierarchy of classes. And we want to be able to put them in an array, a list, a collection, whatever, and iterate over them using a pointer. The pointer should be of the same type as the base class of the hierarchy. But as each object's methods are called, we want each object to use its own methods and not the base class methods.

We saw that in C++ we can achieve this using the "virtual" keyword in front of each base method that is going to be overridden. So C++ implements the Liskov substitution principle, thus is a complete OO language.

Let me give you another example. Suppose we want to write a 2D drawing program. Our program lets the user input a number of shapes like circles, triangles, rectangles, etc. We may implement the program as follows: At first we create a hierarchy of shapes. The base class can be called CShape and would provide basic functionality that all shapes should share. From CShape we can derive the following classes: CCricle for circles, CTriangles for triangles, CRectangle for Rectangles. From CRectangle we may even derive the class CSquare, for squares, since squares are a special case of a rectangle. Then as the user creates shapes dynamically, we can keep these shapes in a list and iterate over them using a CShape pointer. Now, each class may have a method called draw(). Each class should implement this method differently, since a circle is drawn differently than, say, a triangle. Thus, to draw each shape that the user specified, all we have to do is iterate over the list of shapes using the CShape (base class) pointer and call the draw() method of each object (shape). And that is it. Conceptually, our program is complete and one can easily understand it.

Because hierarchies that begin from a base class are common in programs, the Liskov substitution principle guarantees that we can correctly manipulate the objects that are created, even though these objects are created dynamically (so we do not know beforehand where in the hierarchy they belong).

Besides the obvious usefulness of the Liskov substitution principle in such situations, there are two more reasons why scholars insist that this principle is always respected in OO implementations. These reasons are a) polymorphism and b) "is-a" relationships.

Polymorphism

Polymorphism is a Greek word. It means: "ability to take many forms". In OOP, we have polymorphism if we get different responses to the same message.

In Program 6, the statement
```
myBasePointer->speak();
```
resulted in one of three outputs
```
1) This is a Base object.
2) This is a Derived1 object.
3) This is a Derived2 object.
```
depending upon the class of the object the base pointer pointed to.

We had the same thing happening in Program 7. The statement
```
myBasePointers[i]->speak();
```
resulted in one of three outputs
```
1) This is a Base object.
2) This is a Derived1 object.
3) This is a Derived2 object.
```
depending upon the class of the object the base pointer pointed to.

In these cases, the message (method) is the same: speak(), but the behavior, the "form", the output differs, according to the object's class. This situation (in which different objects respond differently to the same message/method according to their class) is what OOP calls polymorphism. And OOP welcomes polymorphism. It is a big part of its philosophy. With polymorphism, we achieve something very useful: we only have to remember something that is easy and intuitive to us and this is the name of the method. Then we can call the method and leave the behavioral details to the specific object.

Relationships

Another reason why OOP purists insist in favor of the Liskov substitution principle, is relationships between classes and in particular, "is-a" relationships.

In OOP, we have two main relationships between classes: "is-a" relationships and "has-a" relationships. When a class is derived from another, the derived class has an "is-a" relationship with the base class, because the derived class "is-a" base class. The derived class is a base class, because it has everything the base class has. If CCircle derives from CShape, then CCircle is a CShape. A circle is a shape; just a more specialized version of it.

The following example will make things clear:

```
class CA
{
    int a;
};

class CB : public CA
{
    int b;
};
```

In the previous example, class CB derives from CA, thus it has everything CA has (int a) and more (int b). Because class CB derives from CA, it is a CA. Thus class CB has an "is-a" relationship with class CA.

When a class has a member from another class, the class that has the member has a "has-a" relationship with the other class, because it has an object of that class.

The following example will make things clear.

```
class CC
{
    int c;
};

class CD
{
    CC object1;
    int d;
};
```

This example shows that class CD has a member object object1 of class CC. Since class CD has an object of class CC, class CD has a "has-a" relationship with class CC.

Of course, a class can be derived from another and have member objects from third classes. Look at the following example:

```
class C1
{
    int a1;
};
```

```
class C2
{
    int a2;
};

class C3
{
    int a3;
};

class C4 : public C1
{
    int a4;
    C2 object1;
    C3 object2;
};
```

In this example, class C4 is-a C1 and has-a C2 and a C3.

Now that we know about "is-a" and "has-a" relationships, we can begin to understand why adherence to the Liskov substitution principle is important.

In Program 7, we have a bunch of objects (100 of them) and we access each one using a pointer to its base class, even though two thirds of these objects belong to a derived class. But even though an object belongs to a derived class, it still "is-an" object of the base class.

Thus, OOP demands that objects of a derived class accessed through a base pointer behave appropriately. They should behave appropriately, because they still "are" objects of the base class. And this is because their class (being derived from the base class) has an "is-a" relationship with the base class.

So, an object should behave appropriately, meaning the right methods will be called at runtime, whether this object is accessed with a base pointer or a pointer of its derived class. It should not matter, because derived objects still are base objects. And this philosophy should be respected in any OO language.

Those are the fundamental concepts of object-oriented programming. To recapitulate, in OOP we strive to create objects that encapsulate their state and expose methods. An object a interacts with another object b by calling one of b's methods. This is viewed as object a passing a message to object b. The data of the message are the parameters that are used to call the method. An object is instantiated from its class. A class can inherit all the properties (data members) and methods (member functions) of another class. We can have class inheritance going many levels deep (class A1 inherits from A2, which inherits from A3 and so on until a base class is reached.) Also, an object should be able to function correctly whether it accessed with a pointer of its own class or with a pointer of its base class.

Interfaces

A popular feature of OOP is interfaces. Before I explain what those are, let me first tell you that C++ does not support them. But it makes up for them with abstract base classes, which are used to achieve the same thing.

To begin understanding the concept behind interfaces, imagine that interfaces are just classes. These classes have no state (no data members). They only have methods (member functions). And these methods are not implemented. Thus, an interface defines a class that has methods with no implementation.

Thus if a class inherits from an interface, it has to provide the implementation for the interface's methods.

That is it.

Let us see now why this is useful. Many times, we want a class to adhere to certain standards. Or, to phrase it better, we want a class to fulfill certain contracts. An interface provides such a contract.

So, I may create an interface named "IContract1" that declares (but does not, cannot and should not define) one or more methods, for example void method1(int) and int method2(void). I may also create another interface named "IContract2" that declares the methods int methodA(int) and void methodB(void).

Now, if a class inherits from IContract1, this class has to implement and expose as public the methods of this interface, namely void method1(int) and int method2(void). If a class inherits from IContract2, the class has to implement and expose as public the methods int methodA(int) and void methodB(void).

I wrote earlier that we will not be talking much more about multiple inheritance. Indeed, only at this point we need to address this issue again. Although scholars have a point that multiple inheritance may lead to programs that are difficult to understand and debug, they do not think so about multiple inheritance when interfaces are involved. Thus, a class may inherit from as many interfaces as needed. Inheriting from an interface means fulfilling the contact that the interface describes. And this amounts to just providing the public methods that interface specifies.

If a class inherits from many interfaces, this only means that this class will have to provide the methods that all these interfaces specify. It is up to the class as to how these methods will be implemented.

It is common to want a class to fulfill certain contracts, which means that we want the class to have certain public methods. Thus interfaces are commonly used. We create the interfaces and they have no code, no implementation whatsoever. Then, our classes inherit from them and multiple inheritance from interfaces does not lead to programs that are difficult to understand and debug (although that may happen in multiple inheritance from classes.)

As I wrote earlier, in C++ we can use abstract base classes to create interfaces. Abstract base classes or abstract classes (for short) are classes that cannot be instantiated, i.e. we cannot declare an object of such a class. They are there just for the sole purpose of us deriving other classes from them. They serve solely as base classes. And they have to have at least one pure virtual method. This method is denoted by appending the "= 0" specifier in its declaration.

```
class CAbstractBaseClass1 {
public:
  virtual double method1(int) = 0;
};
```

The "= 0" specifier has the effect of forbidding this method to be defined in the class. A pure virtual method can only be declared in the derived classes.

Thus, we can see that abstract base classes can certainly be used as interfaces.

S.O.L.I.D.

Apart from these fundamental concepts, OOP purists have defined 4 basic principles that all OO programs should adhere to. These five principles are known as S.O.L.I.D. from their initials. These five principles are: Single responsibility, Open-closed, Liskov substitution, Interface segregation and Dependency inversion.

We have already discussed the Liskov substitution principle, so let us discuss these other four basic principles.

Single responsibility principle. This principle states that a class should a have only a single responsibility. A class should not be responsible for many things, because then this would go against the concept of encapsulation. A class should describe a single entity, a single concept, a single concern and it should encapsulate only the state that corresponds to it. Otherwise, programs will be difficult to understand and it will be easy for programmers to make mistakes.

Open-closed principle. This principle states that a class should be open for extension but closed for modification. What this means is that if you have a class that you would like to use, go ahead, instantiate one or more objects from this class and use them in your program as you see fit. But say that you want more functionality, or somewhat different behavior that what the class provides. In this case, you cannot just go and change the class, because the class code might belong to someone else or because the class code is already perfect and used in many other programs or part of your program. So the class is closed for modification.

Of course, if you find a bug in the class, the owner of the class will have to correct it. The class is not closed for modification that has to do with the original purpose of the class. The class is closed for modifications that have to do with custom requests.

So what do you do now that you have a custom request? Well you can derive a new class from the original class and you can implement the new or modified behavior in your derived class. Because you can derive from the original class, this makes the original class open for extension.

Thus each class (any piece of code for that matter, it is just that OO code exists in classes) should be open for extension and closed for modification. You cannot go and add things to an already existing class, you can derive from it though. This way, code that is known to already work is not touched by additions that need to be made and this provides major help in order to avoid bugs in programs.

Interface segregation principle. This principle states that many smaller and more specific interfaces are better that one larger and more general interface. One reason for that is that no class that implements an interface should be forced to implement methods that it does not need. Another reason is that a large, monolithic interface may easily lead to a large, monolithic program. Taking a cue from the single responsibility principle, we should keep interfaces small and specific, which is the same thing we should do to classes. And in the case of interfaces, small and specific means few methods that have to do with a single responsibility.

Dependency inversion principle. This principle states that higher level objects should not depend upon lower level objects. Instead, there should be decoupled. Dependency inversion is also known as Inversion of Control (IoC). Let me give you an example. Imagine we have a central class that defines the main idea of our program, let us say, the computation engine. Now, this computation engine class may need objects from other classes, like an object that it will use for logging actions, an object for sending notifications, an object for sending emails and so on. But these objects are not central to the concept of our class. Our class, the computation engine class, is very important and all these other classes that may be needed by our class are less important. Suppose we go and implement our class as follows:

```
Class CComputationEngine
{
    //really important data members
    …
    //really important methods
    …
    //helper objects
    CLogging loggingObject;
    CNotificationSender  notificationSenderObject;
    CEmailSender emailSenderObject;
};
```

Then our very important class will be dependent on these three unimportant classes: CLogging, CNotificationSender, CEmailSender.

This way, our class CComputationEngine cannot exist without first having to define these three classes.

But these classes are not only less important but we would also like to be able to replace them with others if we so wished.

Thus, for functionality that is less important and for classes that are less vital to an important class, we would like our important class not to depend on them for its implementation.

Of course, our computation engine class might need to do some logging, but it should not be dependent on a particular logging class. We should be able to define our computation engine class without having first to decide on the particular logging class (or any other helper class) that we will use.

To achieving dependency inversion, we would have to make the more vital classes to not depend upon details and mundane, inferior, helper classes.

There are many ways to achieve dependency inversion. One popular set of techniques goes by the name of "dependency injection".

Please note that although dependency inversion is an abstract concept, dependency injection is a technique or rather, a group of techniques that implement dependency inversion.

A popular dependency injection technique is constructor injection. Let me explain how constructor injection achieves dependency inversion.

Remember that we have a very important class and we also have helper classes. Our important class needs these helper classes in order to fully function and do its work. But we want our important class and all helper functions to be decoupled from each other. If we just go and create "has-a" relationships inside our important class, each to a helper class, then our important class will be dependent on the helper classes, which is something we do not like. In other words, if we go and create data members inside our important class, each an object of a helper class, our important class will do its work, but it will also be dependent on these helper classes for its own definition and implementation. Fortunately, we can decouple all classes as follows.

First of all, for each helper class that we need, we create an interface that the helper class has to implement. Say that we need three helper classes, one for logging purposes, one for notification sending and one for email sending. So, we will create three interfaces, one for logging, one for notification sending and one for email sending.

So we have created three interfaces and each one should specify the methods that must be implemented by the classes that implement each interface. This is obvious, since this is what interfaces are all about.

Now, we already have an advantage. Instead of having only one helper class for logging, we can have many helper classes for logging, each one implementing our logging interface. The same goes for the other interfaces. We can create or obtain as many classes as we want that implement our notification sending interface and we can create or obtain as many classes as we want that implement our email sending interface.

Next, we have to create our important class so that it has a dependence on the interfaces (rather than the classes). Thus, our important class will have a pointer to the logging interface, a pointer to the notification sending interface and a pointer to the email sending interface. And our important class will also have a constructor that accepts as parameters the address of an object that implements the logging interface, the address of an object that implements the notification sending interface and the address of an object that implements the email sending interface. The constructor will accept these addresses and assign them correspondingly to our important class' data members (the pointers just we mentioned).

All that remains, is that at runtime, we instantiate one of our logging helper classes, one of our notification sending helper classes and one of our email sending helper classes and then we instantiate our important class using its constructor and passing the addresses of these three objects as parameters to the constructor. We choose which helper class to instantiate for each interface and we do not have to decide until the creation of our important class.

Problem solved. We can choose at runtime which helper methods we want dynamically. Also, our important class is not dependent on any helper class or any particular implementation.

Someone might argue that, still, our important class depends on the interfaces. Of course this true, but it also desirable. The interfaces are abstractions and we are OK if our high level classes depend on abstractions. We are not OK if our high level classes depend upon specifics, like specific implementations or details.

When you implement dependency inversion, you will find that your program becomes more complex. For example, you introduce interfaces in order to decouple classes. But you gain in the respect that your program is more dynamic and easier to change, if the need arises. Also, it is better structured theoretically. Apart for decoupling, which produces good design and code that is easy to maintain, high level classes are dependent upon abstractions and not upon lower level classes. And this also leads to good design and code that is easy to maintain.

Ok, now let me give you a simple example of constructor injection in C++.

Program 8 – source code

```cpp
#include <iostream>
using namespace std;

void main (void)
{
   class IHelper
   {
   public:

      virtual void doIt(void) = 0;
   };

   class CImportant
   {
   private:

      IHelper* pHelper;

   public:

      CImportant(IHelper* pArgument)
      {
         pHelper = pArgument;
      };

      void importantAction(void)
      {
         cout <<
               "Start of the important action\n";
         pHelper->doIt();
         cout << "End of the important action\n";
      };
   };
```

```cpp
class COneTypeOfHelp: public IHelper
{
   void doIt()
   {
      cout << "One type of help\n";
   };
};

class CAnotherTypeOfHelp: public IHelper
{
   void doIt()
   {
      cout << "Another type of help\n";
   };
};

COneTypeOfHelp oneTypeOfHelp;
CAnotherTypeOfHelp anotherTypeOfHelp;

CImportant anImportantObject(&oneTypeOfHelp);
CImportant
   anotherImportantObject(&anotherTypeOfHelp);

cout << "Testing first object\n";
anImportantObject.importantAction();

cout << "Testing second object\n";
anotherImportantObject.importantAction();
}
```

Program 8 – output

```
Testing first object
Start of the important action
One type of help
End of the important action
Testing second object
Start of the important action
Another type of help
End of the important action
```

Program 8 shows how constructor injection can be implemented. It does essentially what I described earlier in this section. We have a class named "CImportant". At some point it needs to call a helper method named "doIt()". One way to do that is to provide the CImportant class with a member object of a helper class that implements "doIt()". But then, CImportant would be dependent on that helper class.

So instead, we create an interface named "IHelper". And we make the CImportant class dependent on this interface. This is acceptable since interfaces are abstractions, and we want important classes to be dependent upon abstractions, rather than implementations and details.

Our CImportant class has a constructor that will accept as an argument the address of an object that implements the interface.

Now we go ahead and create two helper classes: COneTypeOfHelp and CAnotherTypeOfHelp. We need at least one helper class, but we can create as many as we want. Each is different, but they all support the contract of the interface: they provide a doIt() method.

Then we instantiate the helper classes. After that, we instantiate two objects of our CImportant class. We can see that as late as the point of the instantiation do we have to decide which helper class to use. This is great! Our CImportant class is not dependent on the helper class it will use. We can choose what helper class to use, as we please. CImportant is decoupled from its helper classes (COneTypeOfHelp and CAnotherTypeOfHelp).

I kept Program 8 small and simple. Our CImportant class could have needed helper methods for different concerns. For example, it may have needed helper methods for logging, notification sending and email sending. For each concern (logging, notification sending, email sending) we should create an interface. Remember that an interface just brings together the declarations of a bunch of methods. Thus, a logging interface would encompass the declarations of methods that are needed for logging. And so on, for each concern/interface. Then, for each interface we can create one or more classes that implement the interface (its methods).

Our CImportant class will then use one object from a class that implements the logging interface, one object from a class that implements the notification sending interface and one object from a class that implements the email sending interface. The addresses of these objects can be injected via the constructor of our important class and kept there using one data member pointer for each object address.

So, with constructor injection we inject (pass as arguments and set corresponding data members) the objects (or the addresses of the objects) that implement the interfaces that our classes depend upon. Because the interfaces come "in between", there is decoupling between classes. Our important class only knows about the interfaces it depends upon. Each helper class only knows about the interface it implements. Constructor injection is what will bring all the classes together at the end.

Levels of OO functionality

So, there you have it. All fundamental concepts of OOP have been laid out for you to examine and understand. It is important to understand, that depending on your programming language, programming environment and project at hand, you may have or need only a subset of those concepts. It is not necessary, for example, to implement inheritance or dependency inversion in all projects. It is up to you to decide how much deep into OOP you want to go and how many features of OOP you need for each particular program you write.

And even if your programming environment does not provide any or all OOP features, you can still make do. And it will be easier to program without OOP features now that you know the OOP fundamental concepts, because now you know what you are trying to "simulate".

I will be more specific. Suppose your programming environment lacks the concept of structures. Never mind, you will use parallel arrays (what we did in Program 1). What did you say? Your environment does not support arrays also? Well, that is extreme, but, still, you can use one variable for each attribute (piece of data).

Suppose your environment supports structures, but does not support classes and objects. Never mind, you can still use structures and also create global procedures and functions that accept the structures as arguments and operate on them.

Suppose your environment supports classes and objects. Then you can create classes that contain their data members and methods, so you then are able to use notation such as **object.method(…)** or **pointerToObject->method(…).** Please remember, this is where I drew the line and wrote that you can feel you are into OOP territory when you can do that. And also please remember that I wrote that scholars and purists want even more advanced concepts to qualify a program as OO.

Suppose that you have classes and objects, but your environment does not support inheritance. Never mind, you will create "derived" classes by copying the code from the base class. There is a second trick you can do, as well: change all "is-a" relationships to "has-a" relationships. Thus, in order ro create a "derived" class, you will create a class that has a member object of the "base" class. It is not the same as true inheritance, but it will do.

Suppose that you are able to use classes and objects, but your environment does not support interfaces. You can make do, in C++ at least, with abstract classes. Otherwise, you should just avoid using interfaces.

Suppose that your programming environment supports inheritance, but it does not support the Liskov substitution principle. Never mind, there are lots of ways that you can get correct results when you iterate over many objects and calling their methods. You can have a data member in each object that states the object's correct class. Or you can have different arrays for each class of objects.

Of course, if your programming environment goes as far as to support the Liskov substitution principle, then everyone, including scholars, will agree that you have a truly OO programming environment.

Even then, it is up to you in what way and how much, if at all, you will respect the remaining four S.O.L.I.D. principles: Single responsibility, Open-closed, Interface segregation and Dependency inversion.

You decide the responsibilities of each class, so adherence to the single responsibility principle is a bit subjective.

You decide how many interfaces you will create and what each interface will be like, so adherence to the interface segregation principle is a bit subjective, as well.

You should try to respect the open-closed principle, thus, to implement new functionality, you should try to derive new classes instead of changing existing ones. That is of course, if your programming environment allows you that. A truly OO programming environment supports inheritance and thus allows you to respect the open-closed principle. If your programming environment does not support inheritance, you may use case statements (or if statements) to differentiate between different functionality for different classes. Not nice, but it will do.

Finally, it is up to you if you need to implement dependency inversion. Dependency inversion makes a program a bit more complex, but it also makes changes later on to be easy to do. But for someone to decide if a program needs to implement dependency injection, the criteria sometimes are a bit subjective, as well.

Comparison to other paradigms

The OO programming paradigm in many respects is a continuation of the structured programming principle. Most programs written today adhere to the OO philosophy and are made with OO languages. OOP is very successful.

There are different kinds of programming paradigms and you should study as many as you can. But OOP is by far the most used and most widely known. There are programming paradigms (like aspect-oriented programming) that differ from OOP but do not contradict it; instead they intend to give more functionality to OOP. But there are also programming paradigms that are quite different and, I would dare say, in contrast with OOP. In OOP's opposite corner are "functional programming" and "logic programming". These paradigms remind programmers more of a mathematical notation. Also, they try to be more declarative, which means they try to tell the computer "what to do" as opposed to "how to do it". Functional programming, in particular, is a very popular alternative paradigm and highly regarded as useful, especially among academic circles. This last sentence should not fool you into thinking that it is not for real-world projects. Functional programming's usefulness is clearly shown in many programming projects. In my opinion, if by reading this book, you had many a-ha moments about OOP and its concepts, then the different but very powerful new concepts you will learn in functional programming will blow you away.

Now, let us see where OOP and functional programming differ.

The biggest success of OOP is also its biggest failure: state. OOP is built around the concept of state. An object has state and encapsulates it. This makes programming very intuitive and this is one of the biggest strengths of OOP. But access to this state may lead to concurrency problems. State is not immutable; it can change. Thus access to state should be carefully regulated with locks and this may prohibit high scalability.

Functional programming turns this problem on its head. Functional programming does away with state completely. How does it do this? And what other traits does it have that make it not only useful, but even better than OOP? Well, who knows, perhaps in the future, I will write a book titled "The Fundamental Concepts of Functional Programming". But that should not hold you back, wasting time waiting for non-existent books. Begin, even today, to learn about more programming paradigms and, especially, about functional programming. The more programming paradigms you know, the better you understand where each one lays in accordance with the rest. And the more programming paradigms you learn, the more concepts you learn, and this is always useful.

Thus, time spent learning about programming paradigms is time well spent.

Topics I omitted

In order to keep my analysis succinct, I omitted quite a few things that you will encounter when you research OOP further. Among the various topics I omitted are templates, static classes, static class members, types of inheritance, friend classes, friend functions, operator overloading, virtual constructors and destructors and OO patterns. As you progress into OO, you will learn about these and other OO topics.

Let me quickly give you an idea of what topics you should investigate further on your own.

Templates: Templates are blueprints for classes. Just as classes are blueprints for objects, again, templates are blueprints for classes. So, templates are used to create different classes that share a great deal of similarity. If, for example, we want to create one class that implements a stack of integers and another class that implements a stack of real numbers, we can create a template that takes the type (integer or real) as a parameter and implements a stack of "parameter" things. So, depending on the parameter we pass to the template, a class is created that implements a stack of parameter "things". This way, templates can be helpful, because we do not have to duplicate code, by creating classes ourselves. If we wanted to do the same thing without templates, we would have to create a different class for each type of things we have. And each class would have exactly the same code as the other classes, except for the type. So, in this case, templates are the obvious choice.

Static classes: Static classes are classes that cannot be instantiated. They are useful for keeping global state, global data. Of course, these data are accessed through the name of the static class.

Static class members: Data members and methods can be static as well. If they are, they exist as part of the class and not as part of each object that is instantiated from the class. They accessed through the class name and only one copy of them exists. Static methods can only refer to static data members. Static class members provide a "global" state and behavior for the class, a state and behavior that is shared from all objects that inherit from this class.

Types of inheritance: When we talked about inheritance, in all examples we used the following line of code:

```
class CDerived: public CBase
```

which means that class CDerived inherits (is derived) from CBase. But why is the "public" access specifier there? What does "public" mean in the inheritance process? Can I have "protected" or "private" there instead of "public" and what would that mean?

First of all, yes, you can have "protected" or "private" instead of "public" in the inheritance process. You can write either

```
class CDerived: public CBase
```

or

```
class CDerived: protected CBase
```

or

```
class CDerived: private CBase
```

which gives us three types of inheritance. The difference between these three types is as follows: With public inheritance, the private members of the base class stay private, the protected members stay protected and the public members stay public. With protected inheritance, the public members of the base class become protected, the protected members stay protected and the private members stay private. With private inheritance, the public members of the base class become private, the protected members of the base class become private and the private members stay private.

Public inheritance is the most common type of inheritance used in programs.

Friend classes and friend functions: Fiend classes are classes that are given access to the private and protected members of a class. Friend functions are external functions that are given access to the private and protected members of a class. Friend classes and friend functions are not generally welcome by scholars, because they provide an easy method to undo the effects of encapsulation and access specifiers. If "private" and "protected" access keywords have been specified for a class, they should always be respected. Friend classes and functions go around these restrictions, leading to a less than "pure" OO design.

Operator overloading: One of OO concepts is that a class is like the definition of a new type. A class is a user-defined type. We have talked about this already. Now, since we can define a type, we should be able to redefine the standard operators to work with the objects of this type. Thus, if I create a class for complex numbers, I should be able, if I want to, to redefine the +, -, *, / operators to work with the objects of this class.

Thus, the following will be valid code and give the correct result:

```
// Instantiate two complex numbers
CComplex c1, c2, c3;
// Give values to c1 and c2
...
// Put the sum of c1 and c2 to c3
c3 = c1 + c2;
```

In the previous example, the + operator is overloaded, meaning it has more than one definition. Indeed, it has a new definition for complex numbers.

Another example: If we create a class for strings of characters, we can overload the + operator to concatenate strings. And, indeed, C++ implementations provide a class for strings with the + operator overloaded (redefined) for them.

Another example: The << and >> operators have been overload in C++ to provide input and output. In fact, we used the overloaded << in all the programs in this book.

Virtual constructors and destructors:

These two questions are about to pop up at some point: "Can I have virtual constructors? Can I have virtual destructors?" Well, in C++ you cannot have virtual constructors, but you can have virtual destructors. You cannot have virtual constructors, because when you create an object, you should explicitly know and tell the program exactly what object you are creating. But you can have virtual destructors. When you destroy an object, you want the correct destructor to be called. Thus for an object of a derived class, you would not want the base destructor to be called instead of its destructor.

OO patterns: There are many situations or problems that are

fundamental and of a general nature. For many or all of these problems there already exist implementations that solve them. These are called OO patterns. They are called patterns because they appear again and again. They are common. They emerge frequently. So, implementations for them have been provided by they use of OO concepts (classes, interfaces, inheritance, instantiation, etc.). Something that you would have to figure out for yourself may exist as an OO pattern, which means that it has already been studied by experts and a thoughtful implementation of it already exists and is available. So, you can use it if you like it, instead of having to reinvent the wheel.

By studying OO patterns you get to see how the OO concepts have been used by experts to provide implementations to common situations and to solve common fundamental problems. And you can use the solutions to the OO patterns in your own programs. They are provided for this reason. OO patterns and their OO solutions constitute research that is there to benefit you, the developer, free of charge.

A true story

For the end, I would like to tell you a true story that I feel you may find helpful and it may give you insight at an elementary OOP level.

Here is this true story.

About twenty years ago, a friend of mine came to me and asked for my help. He revealed to me that he had been studying OOP without telling anyone. But he revealed this to me because he wanted my help.

He had an idea about a program he wanted to write, so he began studying OOP alone and in secrecy, in order to write this program.

He told me his idea, what his program should achieve and swore me to secrecy: I was not to tell anyone about his idea. And, indeed, I never told anyone about his idea. And I will not break my oath. But I will tell you that his idea was not an original one, although I do not know if he realized it.

Anyway, he wanted me to help him augment his basic OOP skills, so I began discussing with him (in front of a computer), in order to get a feel as to what his level of understanding was in respect to OOP.

When I created a simple class and I instantiated an object of this class:
```
CMyClass myObject;
```
he immediately said: "Yes, I know this; this is inheritance".

I told him that this was instantiation and that inheritance was another thing:

inheritance is used to derive new classes from existing ones.

But he insisted that since the object had all the members of the class, we could say that the object had in effect "inherited" them from the class. Thus this was inheritance.

I tried my best to explain that even though he was right in his understanding of the underlying "mechanics" of OO, in OO parlance this was called "instantiation" and not "inheritance".

He would not believe me. I tried very hard to persuade him that I was correct and that I knew what I was talking about, but he refused to believe me.

We never talked since, so I do not know if he ever understood what inheritance truly means in OOP.

Epilogue

OOP is the most popular programming paradigm today and for good reason: it is intuitive. It is close to the way we think, understand and visualize the world.

My advice to you is to try to learn at least a few OO languages. For example, try to learn C++, Java, Visual Basic, C# and Smalltalk. See which ones you'll hate and which ones you'll love. Then we can compare our opinions!

If money is an issue, you should not be afraid; almost all languages (and certainly the five I just mentioned) come with free (zero cost) compilers and programming environments.

For example, Microsoft provides a version of Visual Studio (its programming environment) that costs nothing and which comes with support for C++, Visual Basic and C#.

And do not forget: as powerful and widely used as OOP is, there are other programming paradigms as well. Search the internet for "programming paradigms" and try to understand each programming paradigm's philosophy. Especially you should look into "functional programming", OOP's biggest rival. Its philosophy and concepts are quite different and will certainly impress you. But there are no absolutes: each programming paradigm has its pros and cons. And I hope this book helped you understand the pros and cons of OOP, as well as its fundamental concepts.

(This page is intentionally left blank)

About the book:

Where does structured programming end and object-oriented programming (OOP) begin? What are OOP's fundamental concepts and what is the reason behind them? This book will answer these questions and will also give you an insightful perspective into OOP, based on its fundamental concepts. It is likely that you will have many "a-ha moments" reading this book and, at the end, you may even reach a feeling of "enlightenment".

About the author:

Dimitrios Kalemis is an IT professional who specializes in Microsoft products and technologies. You can find more about him by visiting his blog: http://dkalemis.wordpress.com.

Made in the USA
San Bernardino, CA
22 May 2019